BONEMEMORY

 UNIVERSITY OF CALGARY Press

BONEMEMORY

ANNA VEPRINSKA

Brave & Brilliant Series
ISSN 2371-7238 (Print) ISSN 2371-7246 (Online)

© 2025 Anna Veprinska

University of Calgary Press
2500 University Drive NW
Calgary, Alberta
Canada T2N 1N4
press.ucalgary.ca

All rights reserved.

No part of this book may be reproduced in any format whatsoever without prior written permission from the publisher, except for brief excerpts quoted in scholarship or review.

This is a work of fiction. Names, characters, businesses, places, events, and incidents are either the products of the author's imagination or used in a fictitious manner. Any resemblance to actual persons, living or dead, or actual events is purely coincidental.

LIBRARY AND ARCHIVES CANADA CATALOGUING IN PUBLICATION

Title: Bonememory / Anna Veprinska.
Names: Veprinska, Anna, author
Series: Brave & brilliant series.
Description: Series statement: Brave & brilliant series, ISSN, 2371-7238 | Includes bibliographical references.
Identifiers: Canadiana (print) 20240528328 | Canadiana (ebook) 20240528336 | ISBN 9781773856100 (hardcover) | ISBN 9781773856117 (softcover) | ISBN 9781773856124 (PDF) | ISBN 9781773856131 (EPUB)
Subjects: LCGFT: Poetry.
Classification: LCC PS8643.E657 B66 2025 | DDC C811/.6—dc23

The University of Calgary Press acknowledges the support of the Government of Alberta through the Alberta Media Fund for our publications. We acknowledge the financial support of the Government of Canada. We acknowledge the financial support of the Canada Council for the Arts for our publishing program.

Editing by Helen Hajnoczky
Cover image: Dneiper River, Ukraine, March 6, 2001. Photograph courtesy of NASA/METI/AIST/Japan Space Systems, and U.S./Japan ASTER Science Team, https://commons.wikimedia.org/wiki/File:Dneiper_River,_Ukraine_(ASTER).jpg, and Colourbox 61145464
Cover design, page design, and typesetting by Melina Cusano

For Mama and Papa, for the bones & the memories

Contents

I. BONE

Reacquaintances | 3
Evolution | 4
The New York Times reports woman who feels no pain | 5
Waning Identities | 6
Matryoshka | 7
Tender | 8
Kernel | 9
Morning Intimacy | 10
Of wings | 11
Word-house | 12
Woodpecker | 13
Palm Reading | 14
Speaking, speaking | 15
Mouthword | 16
Bernstein's Serenade | 17
Reprieve | 18
Dickinson's Dashes | 19
Two Threads | 20
On the Operating Table | 21
Complex System | 22
Wound at Synagogue | 23
Survivor | 24
Vignettes for Ukraine | 25
A goose lays eggs on the side of a highway | 27
Rattling Bones | 28
Womb-ded | 30
Colon | 31
Afternoon Intimacy | 32
Songs for Ruth | 33
For body with burden | 35
Eyelid | 36
Flesh | 37
Shoes | 38

METAPHYSICAL INTERLUDE

Testimony | 43
Vowels for God – | 44
Prayer | 45
Vignettes for Ukraine: A Prayer | 46

II. MEMORY

Musical Chairs | 49
(O) | 50
Not memory but retelling | 51
Witnessing Names | 52
I | 53
At five years old I forget how to smile | 54
whiff | 56
An olive rolls under the fridge | 57
Breath | 59
Escalator | 60
Narrative | 61
Evening Intimacy | 62
Un-there | 63
Diagnosis | 64
Three Mothers | 65
flowers in war | 66
Papa | 67
Song | 68
Tale from a Train Station, 1941 | 69
Inhalation | 71
Gurgling | 72
Baba Fira's Jars | 73
Erasure in early pandemic journal entries | 75
Birthmark | 77
After witnessing a fallen tree | 78
Trees | 79
Eye exit | 81
Labyrinth | 82
Baking bread | 83
Meanwhile, trauma | 84

Vignettes for Ukraine | 86
Lessons during a pandemic | 87
Five learning English | 88

Notes | 91
Acknowledgements | 95

I. BONE

Reacquaintances

Driving north on Dufferin one early
September evening, my flesh reacquaints
with fall's prodigal bite: bodies of raccoons
and squirrels hugging the soft shoulder
of road, crows guzzling the dead
in their gaping gravemouths. How long
until a body becomes a carcass? A squirrel I nearly
run over but don't   scurries to familiar freedoms –
the pedal's pause a mercy

memoried in the blood
of unhurt generations.

❋❋❋

When her body lay emptied
of story, a stilled dash of bones, I recoiled
from the past tense, the *she was* and *I loved*
required by language's limited
imagination. I turned God out of poems, sneered
at the scar on the horizon
marking the passing   of another day. One night

I spotted a herd of dinosaurs
sauntering through clouds, their fluid forms
a blueprint for release, and thought: nothing
leaves this earth; it just shuffles
its spirit a little: a vultured comfort.

Evolution

In humans

        the soft

                fur of tail

                        hardened

to bone.

The New York Times reports woman who feels no pain

I am throbbing with envy
because she is seventy-one and has steered
her life through the snug grooves of ache-absence
sculpted by a mutated gene. Sure, she doesn't sense
blood oozing from a cut or fingers burning
when removing baked potatoes from the oven. Sure,
these insensitivities tender their own dose
of danger. Sure, pain serves a purpose. Meanwhile

my abundantly-toothed pain gnaws
at my body like a famished god, announces
its chronic presence the way a guest who intends
to stay might announce the need for more linen, chortles
as I shift from here to there to accommodate
the burning in my colon, my eyes,
my knees, these serrated migraines. Earth-sensitive
bones, sticky with hurt. What is this bullshit

about experiencing life fully, pain and all? What kind
of naïve Red Riding Hood do you take me for? About
nine months into the year 2020 in the Gregorian calendar –
that bully of almanacs – the Ge'ez calendar marked
the beginning of the year 2013. How much
I could recover if I retraced my steps to 2013, tiptoeing
backward on an unbruising gradient until pain squatted
hushed in margins, an unborn babe: docile, toothless. Years ago

my father told me *ow* was my most uttered word,
courting pain like a clumsy nightingale. I wonder:
does the woman who feels no pain ever howl
ow? What syllabic gatherings of grievance
break from her lips? What could I know, really,
of the underbelly of her suffering? The same
each of us knows of each. Shadows, shadow.

Waning Identities

The moon is bright tonight,
a plump, pale kneecap.

Neither of us knows who we are.

Matryoshka

Mama keeps a matryoshka doll
from Ukraine in the glass display
in the sitting room: opens it
for the children: reveals
how one rounded body fits inside
another. I know this story: fertility:

the others mama expects
from me. But each doll is also a shard
of mercy: a sheltering of other
within self. This story, then,
gleams with armour,

the figures war-painted
Amazons. A matryoshka
is a band of women sharing,
shielding burdens.

In this one Szymborska poem,
the domestic work of cleaning spills
onto war's stained battlefield.

Each matryoshka grips
both broom and spear.

Each (fertile or not) is sliced with glory, with howl.

Tender

Land
perforated with

theft, as flesh
at wounding –

this cleaved
terrain, this tender

edge
of not yours.

Kernel

Kernel of cooked corn
        seeks out the path most painful
        from mouth to colon, scratches
        its yellow, salt-shawled
        body against mine,
        which is inflamed, a sore,
        chronic gathering
            of bones. Like this,

I unlearn a tongue
        of preference, listen
        for ache murmurs, fold
        across my belly
        like a second skin, a tarp
        to shelter against storm.
                When it arrives,

it is blood and spirit,
        a surrender wolving through me,
        the final wailed notes
        of Andrey Petrov's *Taming of the Fire*.
        Notched with tenderness,
                      I summon

the cradling voice of language:
        to stomach is to endure
        to have guts is to rub
        myself with courage
                      like a salve.

Morning Intimacy

You beside me
in the morning light
is what's still damp
about the earth.

Of wings

One winter morning, when leaves forsake tree
for earth, I glimpse the tangled hairs
of a nest, a home tucked between branch and air
where some living thing laid its care, cooed
and fed and taught to fly. Maybe forgave, maybe
said goodbye. You can tell a pigeon by its wing flap,
a scurried looseness like the shuffling of pages. Folded
in its urban-stained feathers, a manuscript
to inspire or intimidate a young writer. Its first line
a hook, a tether to all winged things – a weight, then.
I, too, am tired. Of restless flight, of virtuous rain
that soaks and shivers what I haul instead
of wings. Again, the risk of breath and song,
weathered because they echo bird. But are not. Are not.

Word-house

Mama is crying on the couch again. Marina and Misha are in the other room. I must be about six, sitting at Mama's feet learning to read. The cover of the book I'm reading pictures a man gripping a bouquet of red balloons. I imagine the balloons carrying the man away. I never consider where the balloons carry him, just the motion of being carried away. We've been living in the new country for half a year now. When Papa returns from work, he brings Mama a sun-yellow *OH HENRY!* to cheer her up. She eats the chocolate bar but doesn't cheer up.

I'm reading aloud from the book with the cover of a man gripping a bouquet of red balloons. Just like Mama reads aloud to me nightly in our first language. When she reads, I imagine words like bricks of a house forming around me to protect me. I want to protect Mama, too. I sneak glances at her while I read. I don't think she's listening, but I'm not upset. I don't know how to pronounce all the words yet, so maybe my word-house is too wobbly to protect her. But I'm learning. I'm cementing bricks, Mama.

Woodpecker

Sound stretches its lungs in the hollow
of the MRI machine: hammer,
car alarm, door knocker, woodpecker

                cleaving to the cavity chiseled from its bill.

Once, on the Isle of Skye, in the interlude
of a storm, we heard the celestial
whirr of whale song. In each sound since

                I have hungered for that windswept coast. *Shh,*

you murmur, a finger cutting vertically
across your face. We (a former we,
the first we) are lying in your bed, eyes

                disarming eyes, wordlost. Here silence grows

its own tongue. And I, still foolish enough
to believe this is love's starved purr.
Weeping turns howl after you leave. What's

                on the other side of this machine: illness

or humdrum? An ear angst presses
against darkness. Woodpecker
drilling one last pocket-void

                into my skull: for years I will gorge on this chasm.

Palm Reading

Last night I dreamt Valzhyna Mort
read my palms and proclaimed
that I have the long fingers
of my grandmother's brother
who was a priest (though nobody
in my family has ever been a priest).

About the future, in Russian –
a language shared between us – she murmured:
ni zhalei sibya (don't pity yourself),
                find ways to survive.

Speaking, speaking

Everything speaks, he offers, his face
a prayer. *Stones, birds, wires, trees.*
If everything speaks, then
what is it saying? The tongue
is a muscle that lifts
out of silence, strokes teeth
like a mother urging children
in the dark wet archive
of the mouth, eyeing the world
for an instant before drawing
back. A river's mouth
is a meeting place, a point where gushing
slows, where one liquid god
pours into another. Sometimes
I open my mouth just
to hear how sound
greets sound. Oh, Philomela,
you taught me the tongue
is not the only tapestry
with which to speak. At the cemetery,
hush is swapped for weeping,
for the coat cradle of arms.
The stones turn their faces away in respect.

Mouthword

Mouths and their twitching

arm ———— so much

a word can- not carry   slips

spits

stills

Bernstein's Serenade

Royal Albert Hall, London, 2018

In the brief intervals
between the movements
of Bernstein's *Serenade after Plato's "Symposium"*
the audience erupt
into a chorus of

coughing
throat clearing
uncrossing
and re-crossing
their many legs
twitching and tuning
their voices, shedding

their boneshells
until the ensuing
interval.

An ear
trained to crowd
notes the hollow
hum of decay
slipped
beneath skinsong:

bones
writhing like strings.

Reprieve

One afternoon I lounge
in an open field
where a lab sniffs
my crotch and a gull
empties on my knapsack.

Small suns (misnamed
dandelions) bend
and unbend their heads
in choreographed prayer.

For hours
I do not wonder
who I am.

Dickinson's Dashes

In the bruised knee of circulation, Dickinson's dashes
are expunged — her buzzing "Fly" too disquieting
for the myth of death (though none of us know it)
promising uninterrupted light. Like this —

I plait your knotted hair into braids,
tell you death comes for other people, *not you,
darling, not you.* Like this —
I dig you a narrative instead of a grave.

Isn't that how we love each other? If love is lamination,
then a dash — this dried blood across the page's knee —
is a knife for every worship. *Cut*, the director calls,
a curt way of unloving. But it is just the ooze of word.

The living, who play hide-and-seek with death,
are endlessly found — and the finding is foul
and necessary. With d — ashes, they dance — buzzing
and buzzing as they let down their braided hair.

Two Threads

1.

My sister shares a story: her friend's uncle, suffering from cancer, wrapped himself in the cold cloak of Western medicine, until he learned of a treatment in India promising a cure. Hopeful, he strapped himself into a sixteen-hour flight and landed on the doorstep of India's scorching embrace – but, soon after arrival, he contracted COVID-19 and died in its lung-clutch. If Atropos – that unpopular Fate – severs the thread of life, sends mortals to the crowded underworld where an old man can hardly find a chair to rest his feet, could she not have spared my sister's friend's uncle the flight to India?

2.

On one flight home, my mother sat next to a woman whose daughter was also a Canadian living in London, and, eagerly, they connected us. We slipped into friendship, meeting for mango lassi, learning our birthdays were three days apart and we lived in the same pocket of the city – until, she died of cancer, so swiftly we never shared that vegan avocado gelato packed in an actual avocado shell (because which of us hasn't had the urge to pretend to be something we're not, steal into a life otherwise fated, whether avocado or *avec* other threads), gelato trickling excess down our wet, warm mouths.

3.

Fate, the clothespin, holds us up as we dry – what thick seas leak from our pinched bodies.

On the Operating Table

In the medical field
there is a surgical procedure known as

resuscitative thoracotomy:

when a patient goes into cardiac arrest –
at death's lip on the operating table –

the surgeon may cut open
the chest

and massage the heart
in a last attempt to bring life

back to the patient.
It only works about 7% of the time

but 7% of the time
someone else's touch saves us.

To touch the heart is more
than a metaphor. It is

to knead
the body of another,

to pull that body back
from a cliff's edge.

Complex System

you
me
youme

Wound at Synagogue

Dress young Wound
in her Saturday best
for synagogue,
where she will stand, swaying
in the pews, pursing
her scarlet lips in prayer,
seeping Torah debris
from her unschooled mouth.

You see,
Wound grew up
in a Jewish-Ukrainian
immigrant family,
her upbringing
buttressed
by anti-Semitism
and scarcities
of food and Talmud.

In this new country,
she opens
to everything, generously
smears religion
on her skin
like sunblock.

She's even
changed her name
to Wanda,
a Slavic word
meaning *wanderer*.

In the sacred house,
she finds her spirit
rubbing against
God's – a gauze
wrapping and wrapping
around the wound.

Survivor

in memory of Helen Berkovitz (1921-2022)

She
        was   introduced
  to   me   as   a   survivor

                but   throughout
    our   acquaintance
      and   later
           our
    friendship

           I   wondered   at
all
      inside
  her that   didn't survive:

the past
    selves   checked
        at   the   door
    marked
        continue

living.

Vignettes for Ukraine

Mama praises herself for pushing for emigration
nearly thirty years prior, because *now* – Mama gestures
at the television, where day and night news from Ukraine
whirls without pause – *our family is absent from that.*

❈ ❈ ❈

I rode an escalator into a Kyiv
metro station just before emigration
in the summer of 1993. I remember
because it was my first escalator,
my first metro station. Now,
on the news, I watch Ukrainians huddle
in the metro stations, birth children
from the privacy of the womb
into war's public, hairy arms. Every year
since turning fifteen, I have longed
to return to Ukraine, if only
to lay stones on the graves
of my grandparents. What Ukraine
will be left for me, or for those
who still call it home?
Who, now, will witness
my grandparents' graves?

❈ ❈ ❈

Recently, after reading
about mass graves
in Bucha, I soundlessly
cried in a stall
of a public bathroom.
A few stalls down
I heard a woman
speak into a phone:

*I
am
so
happy
so
so
happy.*

No other moment
has shown me more
the sea and the shore
of living: the ocean
licking its lips
between us all.

A goose lays eggs on the side of a highway

April's daffodils suckle drops of cloud-grief
in their saffron mouths. What

can the caterpillar know of the butterfly?
A chrysalis unspools toward a wingless thorax:

We, too, imagine it's somewhere up ahead
but the future pursues us: a feral predator

part storm, part sob. *Gravesite*
suggests the dead are a site to behold

and aren't they? When geese lose
their mates, they split from their flock,

smear honks into air, mourn like love
is a bird's invention. In another story,

perched on the side of a highway, a goose
lays eggs while her mate plays sentry.

To an onlooker, this miraculous hatching
might announce centuries of repetition,

feather-swaddled routine; the way
poets – in their boundless-absurd desire to fly –

flock their verse with birds, babbling
and babbling and calling it birdsong.

Rattling Bones

Earth (the tender darling) quakes,

        quivers its upper lip,

    frets as geese

        tending their young. It, too, shields

skin beneath heavy-

        lidded ocean

        eyes – each blink a geography

reconciled to stone.

        If human bodies sport

    pseudo-bones

        for laughter, what flock

of bones throng

    earth and with what mirth

            they rattle.

    Because it cradles

us, we call it mother. But

        every mother

           is someone else's

                    teething child. Not sound

but un-silence, a throbbing pine

                        seeded God-ward.

Womb-ded

(Listen, have you ever imagined
the human body a scar
lacerating earth? I have. Last night
I watched the streets bloom
with figures bounding
home as if hastening
toward a curfewed paradise
and I thought each of them
a bandaged cut, a throng
of flesh throbbing
from womb to) womb, if the grave
can borrow this name.

Womb-ded [woom-ded]:
a way of crouching in the world.

And, oh,
the question of healing – don't trouble
me with such trivialities.
What healing can a scar hope for
that is not another scar? Take
these palms, the way they fissure
in prayer, an idle crevice
yawning between them, mouth
posting murmurs
up to God – what God
could mould miracles
from this small space?

Up close, these wound-walkers
resemble wilting tulips, sunken
heads stirring with penance:
graced   gutted   graced.

Colon

Graceless disease-dancer
stilettoed my colon's lining:
gashes
I learn what ulcerative colitis is the day I
am diagnosed with it:
Do you understand?
The gastroenterologist asks, mopping
his jargon across my
uncertainty assembling
autoimmune immunosuppressed
& other poly
syllables except
undiagnose:

No
I don't understand
how to wade out beyond
this aching how we wait
out survival in decaying bodies
how the word *heal* is embedded
in the word *healthy* & I am now
part of neither
universe: The space
between health &
illness is not
period but colon
porous: porous:

Afternoon Intimacy

Wombed
in this apartment,
jade plant and honeyed
camomile,
book-nudged,

I am sweeping. The couple
one floor below
welcomes
my caress.

Songs for Ruth

1.

I play the mandola of a dead friend.

When I tremolo the double strings,
there are two of us:
her half-a-century-long partnership
with this instrument
and my few weeks' acquaintance
with it.

2.

Ruth's surname was the word
for spring growth: *Budd*.
So, no matter how she aged,
she was always beginning anew.

3.

From the case of her mandola
I inherit the following:
foot stool
tuner
hairbrush
pink lipstick.

4.

The week Ruth died,
I had planned to call her
but didn't, because of every
pressing-unpressing task.

Isn't that how it often happens?

Death whispers
and whisks
away.	Those of us
still being wrung out by life
miss the crossing.

5.

At 96, Ruth told me,
What else could I want from life?
Then she lived another year.

A pink lip of vulnerability.

For body with burden

Virus commutes
from one body to another
like a secret
greeting: illness salutes
a neighbouring, gaping

mouth. I'm on a new medication
that forces my soul out
of my body
like a pine forest felled
to make room

for glass. If we are tender
with ourselves, even a grain
of rice has meaning, even the sheer
body of dust stretching its arms
like a young girl at a concert

not yet burdened by gravity.

Eyelid

Each day the exhausted
   return to openness

to peopled landscape
   to pupiled spectacle.

Seagulls pass, flinching.
   A paranoia of bird.

What it takes to witness –
   to unpeel skin from that other place.

Once on the subway south to College
      eyelid unveiled to witness

         a woman unglove her hand
          to wipe a tear from her mask.

In the moment it took to close from her,
   she surmised what eye had witnessed.

How to endure this shame?
   How to open without harming?

Flesh

A flimsy coat
bunching
at the seams
but making
these bones
bearable, making
them bearable.

Shoes

      Remains of 215 Indigenous children
are found at the site of a former residential school in Kamloops.
      Remains. Euphemism for their bones, for their corpses.
For genocide. How much of this country is an unmarked grave?
      Land carries on reckoning with its history
while government and media scramble to rewrite
      the history of this country.
From Victoria to Halifax, makeshift memorials
      of children's shoes are assembled.
How much of this country is an unmarked grave?
      I recall reeling
from the piles of shoes at the Auschwitz museum,
      bewildered by how clothing could cart absence,
absence cart commemoration.
      There is a travelling empathy museum
(which has been to five continents)
      offering visitors the chance,
while listening to another's story,
      to literally walk a mile in their shoes.
What comes from the reification of metaphor?
      How much of this country is an unmarked grave?
At a conference on empathy in Basel in 2017
      a pair of worn red running shoes takes centre stage.
Feel free to wear these and leave your own shoes in their place,
      the conference organizers explain,
crafting an invitation, not merely a gathering.
      Every day of the conference, I watch
to see if the shoes have been replaced.
      Every day the same red shoes remain untouched on stage.
Nobody takes up the organizers' offer.
      Nobody, is it because we recoil from discomfort?
Nobody, is it because we won't risk losing our shoes?
      Nobody, is it because this is a game
and we are all serious academics suspicious of playfulness?
      No, these are not it. But you know why. You, too,
would not clothe yourself in shoes reeking of rubbered absence.

Empathy, the lie with whom we sit making small talk until decorum dictates we can depart.
　　215 Indigenous children. Makeshift memorials of children's shoes coast to coast.
　　How much of this country is an unmarked grave?

METAPHYSICAL INTERLUDE

Testimony

Somewhere
there is a mouth generous

with opening.
Each lip stirs

in service of its own
secrets. Into the mouth

I shine light
seeking glimpses

of God.
Lightlegible

and damp
God

is trembling.
I leak questions

one
after another:

Where were you?
What

happens after? God answers
nothing:

a tacit testimony, a graced
pair of lungs.

Vowels for God –

I've tried to pray
it away – wrapping
my tongue around
night's womb
so only the invisible
could hear me, though
I wasn't sure if
a God was available
at that hour – or ever.
Somewhere between the first
and seventh year
of praying, I became convinced
an imperceptible
bird (maybe a hawk?)
had thieved the night words
from my mouth, tucked
them into its soft plumage –
a pickpocketing plea vessel
– and winged away.

Since then, my prayers
are handwritten notes,
each vowel underlined
so that God – poor
robbed soul – can see
my cries. Birds
cannot read, I reason,
pressing my pen: *o a e u i y*.

Prayer

Eternal, your spine vertical horizon, your mouth itchy scar salivating with this grace: language-lessness & out of languagelessness language, dragging soiled heels: language the hitchhiker on a road be-tween two cemeteries drawing an arm horizon across grave landscape. How to use words masticated in the mouths of others? Language's archaeology: an underearth

    Eternal polishes & polishes. Bend your spine, Eternal. Let us see you bend.

Vignettes for Ukraine: A Prayer

                          absent

          stones

              f

   r

 o

            m

     its lips
       .

II. MEMORY

Musical Chairs

Memory – unannounced house guest
in distressed jeans and crop top –
kisses each of us on the lips, disrupts
dinner for a game of musical chairs:
at the kitchen table, she shoves

mama, papa, sister, brother, and me
out of our seats, rotates the wooden chairs
outward as if preparing them for a slow
return to trees. Memory plays the Bandura Waltz
(a relic from the old country)

on her dated iPhone, roars *run run run*
as she dashes around the table, slapping
our backs with her sticky hands, knocking
over the gold-rimmed plates packed
with syrniki, spilling kompot that stains

the white linen tablecloth that Mama
will soak through the night in her tears.
Papa, who has spooned music into our mouths
from birth, metronomes our laps
around the table: *presto presto*. But

when the waltz stops, each of us
is eliminated, one by one. Memory –
the swindler – always snags a seat
until she, alone, remains at the table. *What fun! What fun!*
she claps her hands together. From her palms,

the bones of slighter memories
drop, scuffling to the game-discarded
chairs. Each bonememory
scratches a story into its seat with the nail
of a pinky. Each bonememory grows a mouth, a face.

(O)

With history	bitter	on my tongue,	to where
can I return?	Birthed in a city	that no longer exists	self meets self
& they are strangers.	Forgetting	is river's work	is dusk
of underworld.	One eye witnesses	other eye	witnesses. To bear
witness is to bare	witness. (O	I've spent lifetimes	parsing the distance
between memor	y & histor	y, knees cracked	from kneeling
at their naked altars.)	An egg	is a homeland	hosting an assembly
of ancestors.	To remain unhatched,	not arrive	immigrant-thrust
into a country	rubbing out the history	of its people,	absorbing English
until it is intimate	fluency of skin.	Memory-cradled fur:	all else is diaspora, is
			slit.

Not memory but retelling

							After
Chernobyl, there was me,
clambering into a city
450 kilometres south
of cataclysm. At eight months
I teetered on death's
rim, litany of limbs
swelling crimson:
a small, coiled poppy.
That which strove
to enter me – food, water –
I dislodged, recoiling
from the earth-rug
before me. Then a clairvoyant
whose name meant *piano key*
cupped her hands
around jugs of water
and pushed me over
the threshold of the living, adding,
you'll bring joy to your mother's life.

Who am I if I believe this?
Who am I if I don't?

Witnessing Names

Aren't some names heavier than others, leashed to histories
slit with anguish? Auschwitz. Hiroshima. Chernobyl.
Katrina – trauma-soaked syllables.
Names anchored in trespass or shadow. Hefts
one drags from the delivery room

to the hearse. In Ukrainian, the word for name – *ім'я* ('eemya') –
phonetically nudges the Hebrew for mother – אמא ('eemuh') –
which means, name and mother come tangled
in my cultures' languages: monikers trail bodies
like second umbilical cords. Voiced by mothers,

teachers, friends, lovers, names arrive as devotions,
distortions, reprimands, murmurs. Linguistic homes
ribboned and wrapped with meaning: grace, island,
lioness. When I learn his name means *to carry*,
I wonder with what little weights

he has filled his life. "What's in a name?" Shakespeare insists
in a play that unyokes lovers because the name of each
is distasteful to the family of the other. And what of names
that are omitted, written out of stories, unmouthed? Silence
for the fleshly ghosts. Ungravestoned energies deferred

until another world. Named after my grandmother,
whom I never met, I carry my name like a secret heirloom,
an ancestral scar. Names press first scars upon our too small skin.
    On my right ankle, a birthmark shaped like a pink blurry *I* –
a self marked atop self. *I*, our other name. *Aye*, a howled affirmation.

Eye, an iris and pupil: witnessing, witnessing.

I

Language:
a Cubist painting
flaunting
the angles
of the letter
I –

all cheekbones
and blind spots.

At five years old I forget how to smile

Mama took the three of us – Marina, Misha, and me – to a photo studio. *A final memory before emigration,* Mama explained the cost to Papa. Like a puppeteer, the photographer arranged us on the atelier's carpeted platform: positioned our hands, our torsos, our eyes. Then he moved so that the camera was between him and us and commanded, *улыбнитесь* (*smile*).

I tried to lift the corners of my mouth, to smile like I had done countless times in my brief life. But the smile wouldn't come. The puppeteer proffered toys, contorted his face in the wild ways I had only seen in picture books, while Mama urged me to comply in the name of posterity. *I forget how,* I finally confessed.

    The puppeteer laughed and took the photo.

Mama keeps this photo in a plastic sleeve in our first family album, which she stores in the basement of our house in the new country. When I ask for it, she gifts it to me – insisting she has a copy – because that's the kind of mother she is.

In the photo, I am sitting on a chair, stage left. My older sister sits to the right of me, and my younger brother stands slightly behind us at the centre of the frame. I am wearing red sandals, white tights adorned with ribbons, and a pink dress accented by a white flowered bodice. In my hands, I grip a plastic baby doll, which I named Sylva after the Kalman operetta Papa had recently conducted – the last operetta he would conduct for the next thirty years (though he can't yet fathom this expanse).

    And there on my face, instead of a smile, is a scowl.

But this is not an ekphrastic poem; it's a metaphrastic from memory to language, from forgetting – which is a different kind of memory – to the puppet strings of words.

There is tenderness to forgetting, a gift at the feet of all we soon

won't be able to forget:
Marina, Misha, and I,
but especially Mama,
especially
Papa.

whiff

for
some,

   m   e
y   m
  r o

is a

torture
chamber:

mean-
while,

one cloud
smokes

another
in the sky:

how
long

until
we grow

mad
in our

house-
bodies?

An olive rolls under the fridge

I've been thinking about intergenerational inheritance of guilt
in the families of perpetrators,
M. weighs
in a voice message
to me, her Jewish friend.
For example, after the Holocaust

(We are always talking about the Holocaust because of the anti-racism and genocide education program where we met, digging through history in Germany and Poland until we were coated in dirt and spent years writing letters to each other – she in Germany, I in Canada, then both of us in England – toiling to clean the dirt out from our insides.)

but she interrupts
her reflection on the way descendants
of perpetrators
may lug guilt
like an albatross
necked about their ancestral pasts, how shame
as other agony can be inherited,
to remark
that an olive
has
rolled
under the fridge.
I imagine
her balancing
the olive jar
the phone
the memories
now over five years old
and still clawing through
alongside
her empathy
unfurling

across the line and
this olive
compelling enough
to recess the heart's intimate gatherings
as it rolls recklessly
indifferently
out
of
grasp.

Breath

    But that spring morning
during an IV infusion
  when I opened my mouth expecting
air –

    – and nothing came, breath
was all that was left in my book
  of desires.

    To breathe
is to admit the earth,
  nostril-wide, into *I* space.

To breathe is to disclose:

    I need what's outside of me.

Escalator

                At the edge
of the escalator's metal mouth,
      a girl of about seven yanks
her mother's arm, shrieks, *NO, NO, NO,*
              a refrain rubbing
        against the fluorescent lights
      of the department store, wrenches
her body away from the mechanical
teeth, until her mother tenders her own foot
            to the first rung, says, *Look,*
      do it with me. And they step on together,
girl edged with reluctance, mother shame-smudged,
                their bodies descending
                    as marks on ticker tape.

                The first time I rode an escalator
                  was into that Kyiv metro station when I was five,
              accompanying my parents for passports ahead
          of emigration. Mama had weaved a myth
          of autonomously moving stairs,
        and I hungered
          across the city for the manifestation
      of her tale, gesturing
        at every staircase, demanding,
Are these the magic steps? And
      when my parents answered, *No, no, no,*
        amused and exasperated, I didn't believe them, pausing
    on every step – just for a breath – to skim
    the possibility of motion. When
I glimpsed it, I recognized it instantly, its singularity
  gleaming in the summer light. I ran to greet its steely jaws
like a long absent friend.[1]

---

[1] What is the impulse tucked into the folds of skin that propels one person to retreat, shield her bones from even the silhouette of peril, and another lurch her body forward into lesser knowns, into foreign fabric, into the mouths of wolves set with teeth and desire?

Narrative

Last night the heat was stifling. We stayed inside
with air conditioning that chilled our bones. You reached
for me, said one way of living was to let go of narrative.
There is no good, no bad. You kissed my cheek.
I kissed your forehead. There were other kisses
in other places I will not recount in this poem.

Evening Intimacy

The city settles
into autumn's waning coat.
On the balcony, two pigeons
inch toward each other.

I wait until just before
they touch
to look away.

Un-there

after Martha Osvat

I write a friend with news that I've embarked
on a study of oral Holocaust testimonies.
So interesting and so fitting for you, she returns.
I hope it does not break your heart.
And I didn't think it would except

last night I dreamt that the skull
of the person I love most was cleaved
in half and another love
was shot in the Buchenwald camp.
The day prior I had splintered
watching the testimony of a survivor
who spent three days on a train to Auschwitz
packed so tight her skull doubled as byroad
for shifting feet, whose father, later,
was murdered in Buchenwald.

How effortlessly we unyoke from our own lives,
climb into the grief tissue of others, craft homes
in their hurts – like hurtling
through open doors into the arms of darlings.

Six months before beginning my research, I tumbled
into a thorn bush while hiking. As I plucked
the thorns from my skin, one stubbornly
remained housed in my index finger. The swollen
finger needed to be anaesthetized, the thorn
removed with a scalpel by a doctor. She warned
it might disintegrate, plant its tiny specks irretrievably
in my body. But the thorn emerged intact, thick
and sticky, leaving a callus at the centre
of my finger: part foreign trace, part hard reminder
of the *almost* characteristic of healing.

Diagnosis

MAMA: *But she's so young.*

DOCTOR: *Young but defective.*

Three Mothers

Mama tells me a story about her stepmother. She names her *mother* (sometimes *second mother*), this gentle woman who raised her after Mama's birthmother died when Mama was only a few months old. Before Mama's second mother became her second mother, she had another family: a husband and a little boy. One day, this family went horseback riding and the boy fell off the horse, hit his head, and died. Mama says she heard this story of her could-be brother second-hand, that her mother never spoke of her dead son. *You didn't ask?* I probe (I who exhale questions like breath). *I never asked*, she affirms, *because I knew if she didn't tell me, it was something she didn't want to discuss. I didn't want to hurt her by bringing it up.* After this conversation, I go home and think about love. What a love that weathers curiosity, that lives a whole life without touching a wound.

flowers in war

of war
they
too
are
wounded
witnesses

they
shrivel
from
shells
de-petal
from
battle

through
rubble
this
flower
        lower
        over
        ow
        o

Papa

What threads of yourself did you need to sever
to forsake your home – the operetta theatre, the peak
of your career – to tread into this tundra-tipped
land, to slip your tongue
around a foreign language, to shrink yourself
to what an immigrant might hope
for in the howling cavity of starting over?

I watch your eyes, large as moons, the pupils
packed pockets of sorrow. Eyes that close
when you play Shostakovich or Mussorgsky,
suturing our lives with piano keys
like the good surgeon who cuts you open
to betray the prowess of a seamster –
every family needs a doctor, Mama says.

What about a musician? Papa, were your eyes
this large in Ukraine? Take the needle's eye –
the slit hollow, the way it waits to be filled.
Twenty-five years you've rooted yourself to this land
where you've scoured for ways to stitch your loss,
knocking not on doors but on barricades,
loosening your heart from every *no* as from a noose.

Maybe you don't wait any longer, Papa.

Song

Take the words
  sign and *sing*:
shift letters
  and there is music

        (do you hear it?)

if you press an ear
  to this poem – lobe
a fleshy lover furnished
  with heartbeat –

even the dead sing

        (do you hear?)

chirp
chirrup.

Tale from a Train Station, 1941

```
                   With her parents and brother, grandmother (a girl, then) was
fleeing
                        east from the Nazi advance into Ukraine. Tickets in
hand
                            grandmother and her parents paced the train
station
where grandmother's brother had failed to arrive
                                                                  delayed
perhaps by a bike ride or a book's climax
                                                                  losing
(as children often do) track of time, though the repercussions

                             of this loss are seldom tended. I imagine
the tormented
                                              heartbeats of his parents
their weeping
                        and reckoning while clutching their young daughter's
hands.


                            When the train came, they boarded it.


For the remainder of the war
my ten-year-old granduncle
                                                                    hid
at a friend's house
                                                                breathed
through parentless perilous years
                                                                awaited
a family reunion (what thoughts
                                                                absorb
the mind of an abandoned child
                                                                ? What
thoughts
                          absorb the minds of his parents?).
```

After the war they reunited:

each alive   by miracle

each carrying

this familial   history

like a hard lump

near the heart   for generations.

Inhalation

Packing air
into lungs

bulging

like the duffel bags
of thieves.

Gurgling

One river's story:
on the western coast of Ontario, a river named

Penewobecong – meaning *smooth rock*,
meaning *sloping* – was renamed *Blind River*

by the men who judged its mouth difficult
to see. The many-eyed river witnessed

its renaming. History-nicked, it pulsed onward
(a river is busy, after all).

                                              Gurgling

in the throat of the river's rewritten history
is its initial name, refusing to be spit out.

In such a country, a parting of lips
is a translation away from one another.

Not silence but the empty saucer of sound,
a sloping mouth thirsts, continues thirsting.

Baba Fira's Jars

Baba Fira hoards joy
by the jarfuls; arranges
these in rows
like round, unruly
schoolchildren spilling

        from pantry
        to bedroom; pushes
        the divan aside
        to make space
        for her bliss

                basins. As a writer
                might, she stores
                smells, memories, vignettes –
                material for later laments,
                for that one winter (God forbid

                        it come again!)
                        she nearly exhausted
                        all her tears.
                        When the children visit
                        (once in a dozen

                full moons), Baba Fira scolds:
                Open only when absolutely necessary.
                But the children
                want and want.
                Alone again, she cradles

one jar, then the next, purrs
to them: *my darlings.*
At night, by candlelight,
she tiptoes to the bathroom
careful not to disturb

their rest.
On return,
she stubs her arthritic
big toe on a jar wedged
between bed frame

                and peacock feather, swears
                under her sleep-stained
                breath. Tomorrow
                she will empty
                more jars, ready

                                them for filling. *You never*
                                know, she murmurs,
                                marrying herself
                                to dark, again.
                                                        You never know.

Erasure in early pandemic journal entries

March 18, 2020

March 23, 2020

an elderly man   across the street

waved   .

March 24, 2020

sew   cuts in the world

April 2, 2020

he

said.

April 4, 2020

Meanwhile

laughter

April 7, 2020
██████████met██████████grief██████████
██six feet apart██████████████████████
██████████each lugging██████████████████
██████a██████████████████████████████
████████████████████████████████████
██████████

April 16, 2020
████████████████████████████████mouth██████
████open████████

April 24, 2020
██████████████as████████████████████a wound.

Birthmark

Because I am human,
I desire more
than serenity slipping
its arms about my waist,
as a child unschooled
in the breach
blossoming
between bodies
that were once
the recipients
of nightly confessions
of love.

Meanwhile, borders,
holding up
their floor-length skirts,
are shifting after war.
Each dances
with the coquetry
of new love,
though old love
– the perennially
flushed fool –
has yet
to be forgotten,
though old love
is a gash at the thigh
new love mistakes
for a birthmark.

After witnessing a fallen tree

About wailing, you say little. Instead
you gesture at the fallen tree:

in the forest, living and dying play out
in the space of a human palm: dead trees

lie like prayer rugs at the feet of the living.
Conversely, we make an event of death,

moulding ceremonies from loss, sitting shiva
on minute stools, dressing to match metaphors

of mourning. A friend visits her ailing
grandmother, tells of the passing in the next room:

I could hear the wailing. To intrude
upon each other, even with ears,

is a way of the living. But the dead
are tucked into the earth, where overhearing yields

to packed soil.
In a testimony I watch, a Holocaust survivor

reads graves as proof of living. A grave
is not merely a disposal for the body:

it's a vessel to document the marriage of grief
and memory, to tender the dignity of burial.

On its way groundward, one tree
sometimes drops on the shoulders of another.

Occasionally, the dying tree splits the living tree
in half. With the parts it can, the living tree

carries on swaying: a tree's prayer
for the blooming-decaying earth, for its wails.

Trees

This month shelved several loved ones into earth.

❋❋❋

I used to live on a street winding
up to a cemetery atop a hill.
In that city the wind howled and once
I flipped the heat on
in June. How to tell you this story?
The tulips opened and wilted
in the span of a week.
A hurricane lifted the pavement.

❋❋❋

I am not home for any of the funerals.
Twenty minutes before the funeral for an uncle
instrumental in my family's emigration,
my sister texts, asking for a poem I've written
that she can read as part of his eulogy.
Frustrated, I respond I don't have poems ready on command

but search for one anyway.

After removing several potentially offensive lines,
I send her a poem about dying trees.

❋❋❋

In the city with the howling wind
the house shook
the night of the hurricane.
I considered sleeping
on the bathroom floor
because the aged maple tree
outside the bedroom window

– like a devout disciple –
bowed and bowed to the ground.

              Afterward,
for months, shingles
lined the pavement and trees
blanketed roads. Many of us
were without power for a week,
without shade for years.

Eye exit

after Paul Celan

The stone – "behind the eye," a translation of Paul Celan's "Vinegrowers" murmurs. To weigh a stone is no easy thing. Roll it from one present to another: borderless space between past and future. Out of the stone grow oughtflowers, morning glories, grapes. In one crack, a gasp behind a ribcage. Language takes and takes until it is storehouse for memory. A woman in an art workshop confesses, *Before I broke my arm, I was learning calligraphy.* The eyelash, too, is a learned thread, a vine alchemied into a tiny spine holding up a lid. Blink blink. The scarred silence after penance. An archaeologist at the end of days, shovelgasped, brushing and brushing the dirt from their skin

– spitting out the eye.

Labyrinth

after Jacob Rosenberg

In the poem, the Holocaust survivor
invokes a labyrinth as he attempts
to surface a language with which
to compass his past
                (to say *unspeakable*
is to dismiss, to erect a door, to declare,
you, word-bred, history-coddled soul,
can't enter here
                (no,
even Ariadne's thread disintegrates
in this labyrinth, where a sister hangs
herself on barbed wire after learning
her child was gassed
                (how to depart
that world for this one, with its frivolity
and other griefs? "I don't know,"
the survivor concedes and raises
his hands with a shrug
                (years ago,
on a genocide education program,
while weaving through the barracks
in Auschwitz, my right arm
went numb, veered away from
sensation in a way I experienced
neither before nor since
                (sometimes
our bodies articulate
what our language cannot
                (but
my Auschwitz, swarming
with exhibits and restless tourists,
is not his Auschwitz, my language
not his language
                (I am not
talking about Polish or English,
rather about shadow, about loose
bits of frayed thread)))))))

Baking bread

Under
my knucklebones
I knead
shame.
It catches
in a fissure,
burrows in.

Meanwhile, trauma

1.

Packing Ukraine
into a three-suitcase memory
in 1993, we held

& unheld our culture
at the gate, on the plane, years later when I travelled &
someone asked where home was & I answered Canada without

pausing. We fled
anti-Semitism, lack of food & opportunity:
though this was far from being the only narrative,

we were permitted entry. There are different closures:
wounds, borders, bodies – in front of Kafka's gatekeeper
the pain of unwelcome proliferates.

2.

The day of the 2016 U.S. election
I was living in Washington, D.C., researching
Holocaust testimonies, unravelling

in the grief of others.
Outside my window
the Rosslyn Twin Towers canvassed

the live projection of presidential results.
By morning, silence burden-stretched
across the city:

we wept, prepared
our bones while democracy limped in the streets. Here –
& at other shores

there were no firebreaks & drowning
was the gravest
displacement of the body.

3.

I was back in Toronto
in 2020 when earth's gravesite
widened. Our bodies bent

into closures, anchored
by our own borders.
Leaking,

I forgot
what it felt like
to be held by my mother. Meanwhile, trauma

picnicked indoors & spat while speaking.
Drenched, we witnessed its ability
to enter anywhere.

Vignettes for Ukraine

– our family is absent

       metro stations

                              if only
to lay stones

      mass graves

the   sea   and   the   shore

Lessons during a pandemic

The upstairs neighbours laugh through the vents. Meanwhile, I am virtually teaching Elie Wiesel's *Night*. Some students have faces, others are little black boxes on the screen. During the question period, when I say, *ask anything*, one student says, *how do we deal with this grief?* I should have said, *anything but that*. I stumble through an answer: *I think it's okay to be sad. It's okay to align yourself with sorrow.* Then I turn the question (this mouth weapon) back at them: *How do you deal with grief?* Some students speak of sharing their thoughts with loved ones, others of writing or drawing. *What helps me*, I finally say, *is being able to hold the book and let it go simultaneously* (never mind I don't do this very well). As we say our goodbyes, the boxes dwindling, I add (maybe stupidly), *when you rejoin the world, don't forget about the laughter.*

Five learning English

I am five, learning English
from picture books and kindergarten teachers.
The teachers are cross whenever I tap them
to summon their attention.
         Use your words, they say.

But when I do, they say,
No, not those words. English.
English. English. English
         protruding its tongue
           to slurp homeword out of me.

      At five *my name is Anja*
because Papa, registering me for school,
spelled my name
after its Slavic pronunciation, *Anya*.
But everyone voices the 'j' and I am Anja.

Anja, say present.
Anja, cross your legs.
Anja, spell your name.
English – the sovereign – refuses this consonant silence,
      and I am silenced by a name I cannot recognize.

When I absorb the alphabet
– pencil tracing rounded bellies of letters –
      I abandon drawing, scratch *abcdefg*
across notebooks, our kitchen table, the peeling walls
of the apartment my parents have rented

with money they do not have:
                             abcdefg:

letters but also notes:
music   chant
            spell.

※※※

Nearly thirty years later, I trace the bones
of words in dictionaries:
        riverine, clandestine, iridescent:
words whose hair I part again and again,
like curtains revealing further curtains.

In every term I mispronounce, I am five,
learning English. In every poem I write –
not with fingers but fists –   I am Anja, learning
        English, cowering under the heft of its appetite,
coveting under the heft of my appetite.

NOTES

"*The New York Times* reports woman who feels no pain" responds to the following article: Murphy, Heather. "At 71, She's Never Felt Pain or Anxiety. Now Scientists Know Why." *The New York Times*, 28 March 2019.

"Matryoshka" alludes to Wisława Szymborska's poem "The End and the Beginning": Szymborska, Wisława. "The End and the Beginning." *Poems, New and Collected*, translated by Stanisław Barańczak and Clare Cavanagh, Harcourt, Inc., 1998, p. 228-29.

"Kernel" references Andrey Petrov's Overture to the movie *Taming of the Fire*, as arranged by Alexander Veprinskiy.

"Speaking, speaking" is for B.W. Powe.

"Bernstein's Serenade" references Leonard Bernstein's *Serenade after Plato's "Symposium"* as heard by me at the Royal Albert Hall in London, UK in 2018.

"Dickinson's Dashes" alludes to the practice of homogenizing Emily Dickinson's dashes upon publication. This poem also references Dickinson's poem [465]: Dickinson, Emily. "[465]: I heard a Fly buzz – when I died –." *Essential Dickinson*, selected by Joyce Carol Oates, HarperCollins, 1996, pp. 31-2.

"Two Threads" is for and in memory of Christine Hone-Buske, the friend in the second half of this poem, who passed away on May 22, 2019.

"Complex System" and "Narrative" are for Firas Momani.

"Survivor" is for Helen Berkovitz, who became a dear friend after we collaborated on her memoir for the Sustaining Memories Project. See https://memoirs.azrielifoundation.org/exhibits/sustaining-memories/helen-berkovitz/. Helen passed away on April 9, 2022.

"Songs for Ruth" is for Ruth Budd, a wonderful musician and friend with whom I played in the Toronto Mandolin Orchestra for fifteen years. Ruth passed away on June 30, 2021.

"Shoes" confronts the horrific history of the residential school system in Canada. In 2021 Tk'emlúps te Secwépemc hired a ground-penetrating radar expert, whose findings showed remains of Indigenous children buried at the former Kamloops Indian Residential School. This news was reported widely across Canada and the world. See, for example, https://www.cbc.ca/news/canada/british-columbia/tk-emlúps-te-secwépemc-215-children-former-kamloops-indian-residential-school-1.6043778.

"Prayer" alludes to Paul Celan's poem "Tenebrae."

"Musical Chairs" mentions the Bandura Waltz, a traditional Ukrainian folk tune.

"Witnessing Names" and "Three Mothers" are for Mama. "Witnessing Names" references William Shakespeare's *Romeo and Juliet*.

"At five years old I forget how to smile" refers to Emmerich Kálmán's operetta *Die Csárdásfürstin*.

"An olive rolls under the fridge" is for Marika Pietsch. This poem alludes to the Mark and Gail Appel Program in Holocaust and Antiracism Education, which Marika and I were participants of in 2013.

"Un-there" is for Martha Osvat. The poem is in response and includes references to Osvat's interview with the Visual History Archive. Citation: Osvat, Martha. Interview 32046. Interview by Sandy Hoffman. Visual History Archive, USC Shoah Foundation, July 31, 1997. Accessed Dec. 1, 2020. The first stanza of "Un-there" includes words from my friend Laura Wiseman.

"Papa" is, of course, for Papa.

"Trees" alludes to Hurricane Fiona, which I experienced in Sydney, Cape Breton in September 2022.

"Eye exit" borrows a line from Paul Celan's "[Vinegrowers]": "the stone behind the eye" (translated by Pierre Joris in *Breathturn into Timestead: The Collected Later Poetry*. Farrar, Straus and Giroux, 2014).

"Labyrinth" is for Jacob Rosenberg. The poem is in response and includes references to Rosenberg's interview with the Visual History Archive. Citation: Rosenberg, Jacob. Interview 20686. Interview by Ena Burstin. Visual History Archive, USC Shoah Foundation, Sept. 9, 1996. Accessed Feb. 3, 2021.

"Meanwhile, trauma" is for my parents. Thank you for uprooting your lives in the hopes that your children would have better ones. This poem alludes to Franz Kafka's parable "Before the Law."

"Lessons during a pandemic" is for my students in *EAC720: Literature of the Holocaust* at Seneca College in the summer of 2020. All quotes are approximate.

ACKNOWLEDGEMENTS (for prints)

The poems "Not memory but retelling," "Un-there," "flowers in war," "Palm Reading," "Erasure in early pandemic journal entries," "Speaking, speaking," "Dickinson's Dashes," "Eye exit," "For body with burden," "Lessons during a pandemic," and "Song" were first printed in the chapbook *Stone Blossom* (Anstruther Press, 2022), with appreciation to Jim Johnstone.

The poems "Tender," "Afternoon Intimacy," "I," "Inhalation," and "Baking bread" were first printed, without titles, in the chapbook *Spirit-clenched* (Gap Riot Press, 2020), with appreciation to Kate Siklosi and Dani Spinosa.

The poem "Tender" was reprinted in the anthology *Immigrant Voices in the Pandemic* (Solis Press, 2023), with appreciation to Roxana Cazan and Domnica Radulescu.

The poems "Survivor," "Shoes," "Tale from a Train Station, 1941," "Labyrinth," and "Lessons during a pandemic" were recorded for the public talk "Haunted Words: Holocaust Literature at the Intersection of Genres" at the University of Toronto's Anne Tanenbaum Centre for Jewish Studies. The talk is available on YouTube: https://youtu.be/6ruoEooUsA8?si=Cvp8p_L3b9_osPyj.

Thank you to the editors of the following journals, where poems from this collection first appeared, often in prior iterations:

8 Poems: "For body with burden"
The Angle: "Gurgling"; "Lessons during a pandemic"
Arc Poetry Magazine: "Two Threads"
Canadian Literature: "Witnessing Names"
Contemporary Verse 2: "Vignettes for Ukraine" (the version in the "Bone" section of this book)
Hamilton Arts & Letters: "Speaking, speaking" (reprinted in *New Explorations: Studies in Culture and Communication*)
Holocaust Studies: A Journal of Culture and History: "Un-there"; "Labyrinth"
League of Canadian Poets' Poetry Pause: "Afternoon Intimacy" (first printed in *Spirit-clenched* (Gap Riot Press)); "Evening Intimacy"

Magine: Unama'ki / Cape Breton's Literary Magazine: "Of wings"
Not Very Quiet: "An olive rolls under the fridge" (reprinted in *Not Very Quiet: the anthology*. Eds. Moya Pacey and Sandra Renew. Recent Work Press. 2021)
Parentheses Journal: "Matryoshka"
talking about strawberries all of the time: "Evolution"; "Waning Identities"; "Mouthword"; "whiff"; "flowers in war"
The /tɛmz/ Review: "Kernel"; "On the Operating Table"
untethered magazine: "(O)"
WordCity Monthly: "Tender" (first printed in *Spirit-clenched* (Gap Riot Press))

Prior iterations of these poems also received the following distinctions:

"Vignettes for Ukraine" (the version in the "Bone" section of this book) was a finalist for the Ralph Gustafson Poetry Contest (2024)
"(O)" was shortlisted for the *Austin Clarke Prize in Literary Excellence* (2023)
"Kernel" was a finalist for *Best of the Net* (2022)
"Not memory but retelling" received Honourable Mention for *Arc Poetry Magazine*'s June *Award of Awesomeness* (2021)
"Shoes" was shortlisted for the *Austin Clarke Prize in Literary Excellence* (2021)

ACKNOWLEDGEMENTS (for people)

Thank you to my editor, Helen Hajnoczky, for the close and deeply thoughtful attention to this collection; it's a gift for a work to be given such care. Thank you to everyone at the University of Calgary Press and the Brave & Brilliant series – including Brian Scrivener, Aritha van Herk, Helen Hajnoczky, Alison Cobra, and Melina Cusano – for believing in this collection and bringing it into the world. Thank you to my colleagues at the University of Calgary for welcoming me with open arms; I am endlessly grateful to be among – and in awe of – your kindness and creativity. Thank you to the generous first readers of some of these poems, whose feedback was invaluable in shaping the collection: Jim Johnstone, Sarah Jensen, Renée Jackson Harper, Meryl Borato, J.S. Porter, B.W. Powe, Doris Bergen, Karen Quevillon, Jay Millar, Joy David, Maya C. Popa, Kate Siklosi, and Dani Spinosa. Thank you, always, to Andy Weaver, Sara Horowitz, Julia Creet, B.W. Powe, and Doris Bergen, who have helped shape my writing and thinking. Thank you to Ilya Kaminsky for his early support of these poems, his work in Ukraine, and his astonishing writing and thinking.

Thank you to the family and friends who have loved and cared for me during the process of writing this book, especially Mama, Papa, Marina, Misha, Jeff, Emma, Tiffany, Irina, Marina, Asha, Meryl, Sarah, B.W., Marika, Sean, Lee-Anne, and the many others not listed here. To the little ones I adore and who boundlessly inspire me: Sam, Benji, Ellie, Jacob, Ava, and Jonah. And to Firas, my sweetheart: thank you for your unconditional love, acceptance, and support. Our love is the poem I have always longed to write.

Photo Credit: Anna Veprinska

ANNA VEPRINSKA is the author of *Empathy in Contemporary Poetry after Crisis*. She was a finalist in the Ralph Gustafson Poetry Contest, has been shortlisted for the Austin Clarke Prize in Literary Excellence, and received an Honourable Mention from the Memory Studies Association First Book Award. She is an assistant professor in the Department of English at the University of Calgary.

 **BRAVE & BRILLIANT SERIES**

SERIES EDITOR: Aritha van Herk, Professor, English, University of Calgary
ISSN 2371-7238 (PRINT) ISSN 2371-7246 (ONLINE)

No. 1 ·	*The Book of Sensations* | Sheri-D Wilson
No. 2 ·	*Throwing the Diamond Hitch* | Emily Ursuliak
No. 3 ·	*Fail Safe* | Nikki Sheppy
No. 4 ·	*Quarry* | Tanis Franco
No. 5 ·	*Visible Cities* | Kathleen Wall and Veronica Geminder
No. 6 ·	*The Comedian* | Clem Martini
No. 7 ·	*The High Line Scavenger Hunt* | Lucas Crawford
No. 8 ·	*Exhibit* | Paul Zits
No. 9 ·	*Pugg's Portmanteau* | D. M. Bryan
No. 10 ·	*Dendrite Balconies* | Sean Braune
No. 11 ·	*The Red Chesterfield* | Wayne Arthurson
No. 12 ·	*Air Salt* | Ian Kinney
No. 13 ·	*Legislating Love* | Play by Natalie Meisner, with Director's Notes by Jason Mehmel, and Essays by Kevin Allen and Tereasa Maillie
No. 14 ·	*The Manhattan Project* | Ken Hunt
No. 15 ·	*Long Division* | Gil McElroy
No. 16 ·	*Disappearing in Reverse* | Allie McFarland
No. 17 ·	*Phillis* | Alison Clarke
No. 18 ·	*DR SAD* | David Bateman
No. 19 ·	*Unlocking* | Amy LeBlanc
No. 20 ·	*Spectral Living* | Andrea King
No. 21 ·	*Happy Sands* | Barb Howard
No. 22 ·	*In Singing, He Composed a Song* | Jeremy Stewart
No. 23 ·	*I Wish I Could be Peter Falk* | Paul Zits
No. 24 ·	*A Kid Called Chatter* | Chris Kelly
No. 25 ·	*the book of smaller* | rob mclennan
No. 26 ·	*An Orchid Astronomy* | Tasnuva Hayden
No. 27 ·	*Not the Apocalypse I Was Hoping For* | Leslie Greentree
No. 28 ·	*Refugia* | Patrick Horner
No. 29 ·	*Five Stalks of Grain* | Adrian Lysenko, Illustrated by Ivanka Theodosia Galadza
No. 30 ·	*body works* | dennis cooley
No. 31 ·	*East Grand Lake* | Tim Ryan
No. 32 ·	*Muster Points* | Lucas Crawford
No. 33 ·	*Flicker* | Lori Hahnel
No. 34 ·	*Flight Risk* | A Play by Meg Braem, with Essays by William John Pratt and by David B. Hogan and Philip D. St. John, and Director's Notes by Samantha MacDonald
No. 35 ·	*The Signs of No* | Judith Pond
No. 36 ·	*Limited Verse* | David Martin
No. 37 ·	*We Are Already Ghosts* | Kit Dobson
No. 38 ·	*Invisible Lives* | Cristalle Smith
No. 39 ·	*Recombinant Theory* | Joel Katelnikoff
No. 40 ·	*The Loom* | Andy Weaver
No. 41 ·	*Bonememory* | Anna Veprinska

www.ingramcontent.com/pod-product-compliance
Lightning Source LLC
Chambersburg PA
CBHW050033090426
42735CB00022B/3468